Round the...
with...
PEAK DI...
CYCLING · Vol One.

by
Graham Kirkby

Maps and photographs by John N. Merrill
© Walk & Write Ltd, 1999.

The Peak District Cycling Series

1999/2000

Produced by a member of
THE GUILD OF MASTER CRAFTSMEN

Happy Walking International Ltd

**Happy Walking International Ltd.,
Unit 1, Molyneux Business Park,
Whitworth Road,
Darley Dale, Matlock, Derbyshire.
DE4 2HJ
Tel/Fax 01629 - 735911
email - john.merrill@virgin.net**

Printed, bound, marketed and distributed by Happy Walking International Ltd.

© Text, - Graham Kirkby 1999
© John N. Merrill/Walk & Talk Ltd 1999
© Maps - John N. Merrill/Walk & Write Ltd. 1999.

First Published - October 1995
This reprint - August 1999

ISBN 1 874754 54 3

British Library Cataloguing-in-Publication Data.
A catalogue record for this book is available from the British Library.

Please note - The maps in this guide are purely illustrative. You are encouraged to use the appropriate 1:50,000 O.S. map.

Meticulous research has been undertaken to ensure that this publication is highly accurate at the time of going to press. The publishers, however, cannot be held responsible for alterations, errors or omissions, but they would welcome notification of such for future editions.

Typeset in AGaramond - bold, italic and plain 10pt, 14pt and 18pt.

Printed by - Happy Walking International Ltd.
Designed and typset by Walk & Write Ltd.

Cover photograph - Sheepwash Bridge, Ashford in the Water, by John N. Merrill © Walk & Talk Ltd.

Cover design© Walk and Write Ltd. 1998.

ACKNOWLEDGMENTS

I would like to thank my mother for her patience, and Peter for helping check the final details.

ABOUT THE AUTHOR

He was born in 1944, and since being fourteen years old has lived close to the Peak District. Before that he lived in Hull, and regularly cycled to Hornsea, on his Raleigh fitted with straight handle bars and Sturmey Archer gears. Cycling has continued to be a part of his life. Other interests include walking, especially challenge walks, road and fell running and orienteering.

CONTENTS

YOUTH HOSTELS

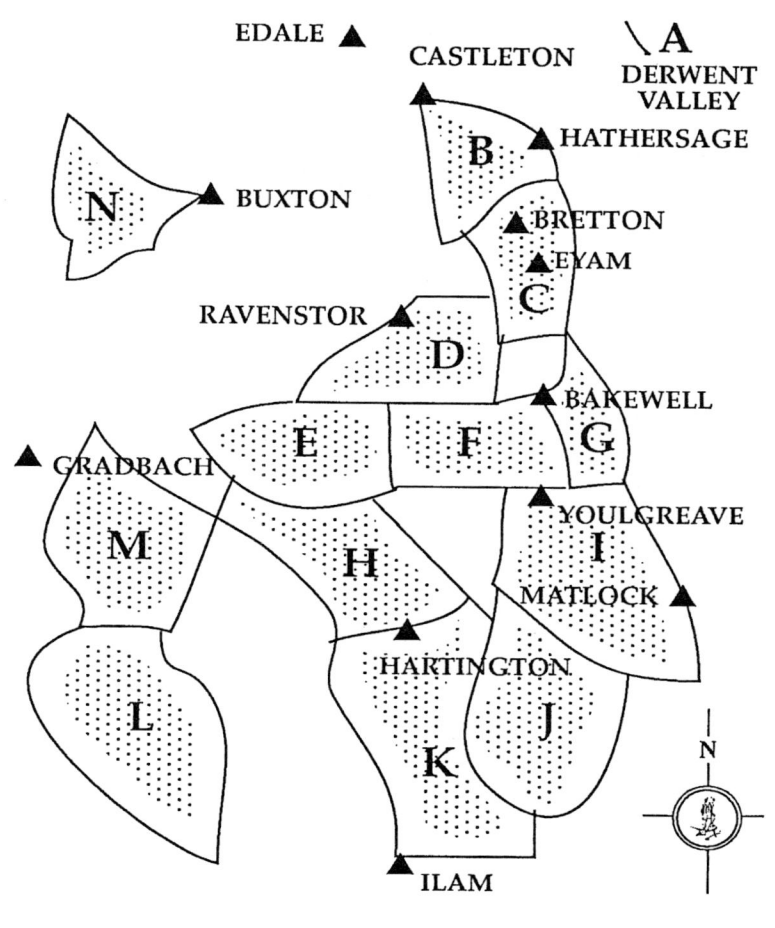

Bakewell	01629 - 812313	
Bretton	01742 - 884541	
Buxton	01298 - 22287	
Castleton	01433 - 20235	
Edale	01433 - 670302	
Eyam	01433 - 30335	
Gradbach Mill	01260 - 227625	
Hartington Hall	01298 - 84223	
Hathersage	01433 - 50493	
Ilam	0133529 - 212	
Matlock	01629 - 871803	
Ravenstor	01298 - 871826	
Youlgreave	01629 - 636518	

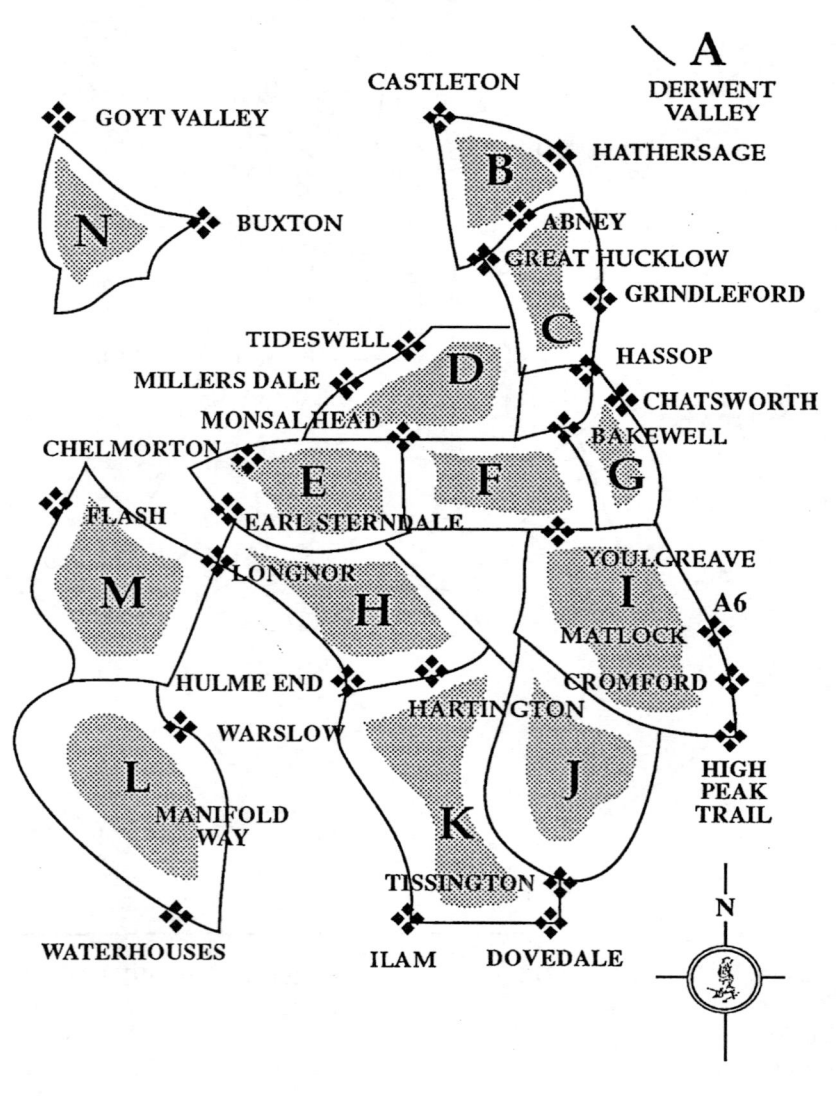

INTRODUCTION

There are no flat roads in the Peak district, but this is an attempt to guide the cyclist along some of the flatter routes. There were several requirements for this book.

1. *Flattest routes possible.*
2. *Quiet roads.*
3. *Beautiful views.*
4. *Manageable length.*
5. *Circular routes.*
6. *Car parking nearby.*
7. *Routes to link up.*
8. *Good road surface.*

This book is for people who have explored the cycle trails, built up a degree of fitness, and wish to explore further. The routes can be linked together making it possible to cycle the length and breadth of Peak District on fairly flat roads. The heading indicates the starting point which is usually from car parks, generally near the most difficult section, so that the worst can be got over early. Distances have been calculated by time and reflect the nature of the terrain. The direction of the routes take the cyclist down the steeper hills. The pubs have been included in the route description as they make good landmarks. Some vantage points are included, which, combined with the excellent scenery of the Peak District, the Cycle Trails and the Youth Hostels make this guide an ideal companion.

Happy cycling!

Graham.

Route A - DERWENT VALLEY

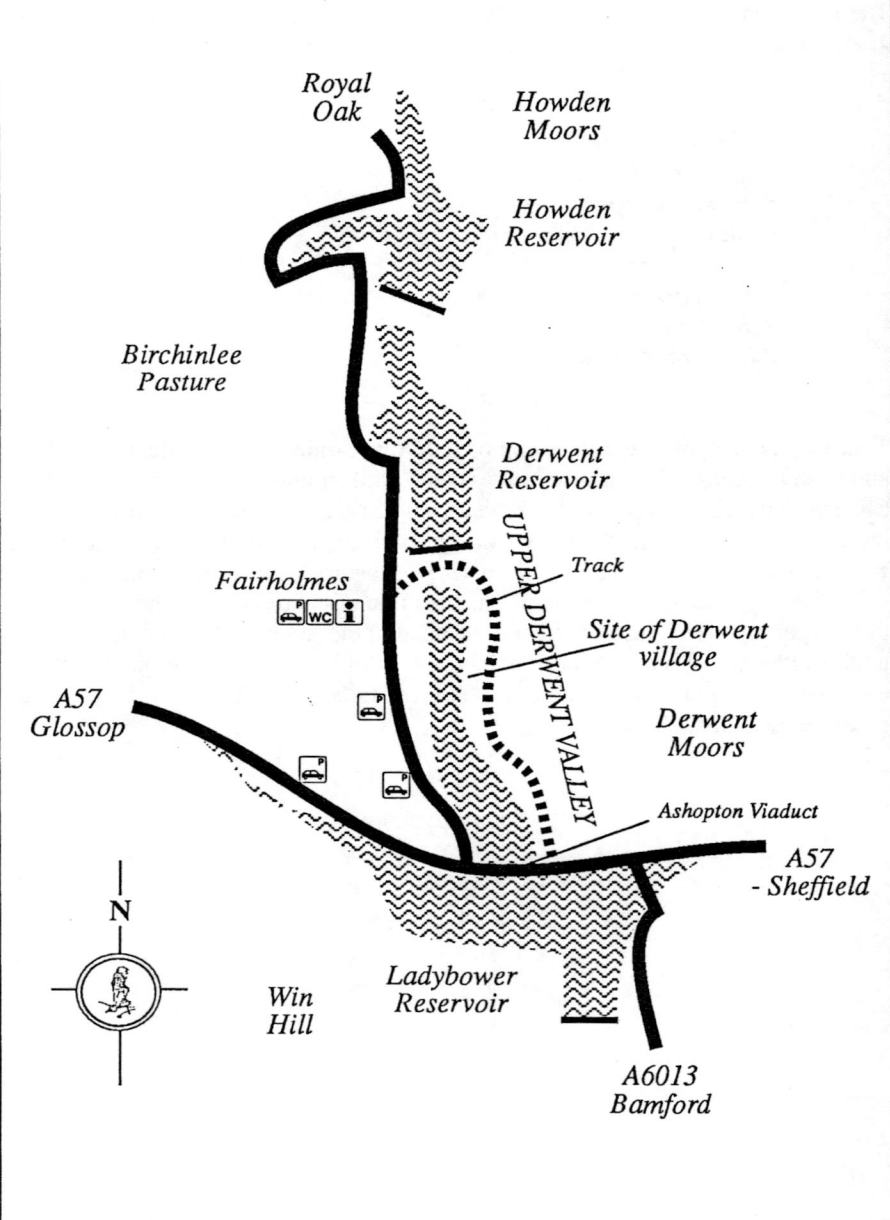

DERWENT VALLEY (A)

There is only one road in the Derwent Valley so a route description is not really needed. There are not many cars, and at weekends and bank holidays it is closed to traffic, except for residents, making it safe for the cyclist.

People have probably lived in the Derwent valley since early man came this far north, and now the remains of two villages lie under water. The Dam Busters trained there, and at the end of the valley is an oak tree called the Royal Oak, planted by King George VI on 25th September 1945 to commemorate the end of the war. In these fifty years, it has only grown to perhaps twelve feet tall, reminding us how long trees take to reach maturity, and our responsibility to look after them in this age of deforestation

The valley is steeply sided, wooded and sheltered from wind. Rhododendrons border the road which is fairly flat, undulating slightly as it leaves the waters edge, giving fresh vistas at each new turn. It is ideal for picnics. There are several car parks, a cycle hire, and a small cafe.

For a moving account of the lost villages of Ashopton and Derwent read the excellent book by Vic Hallam called the Silent Valley, published by Sheaf Publishing.

Ashopton viaduct, one January morning.

9

Route B - CASTLETON - 18 MILES

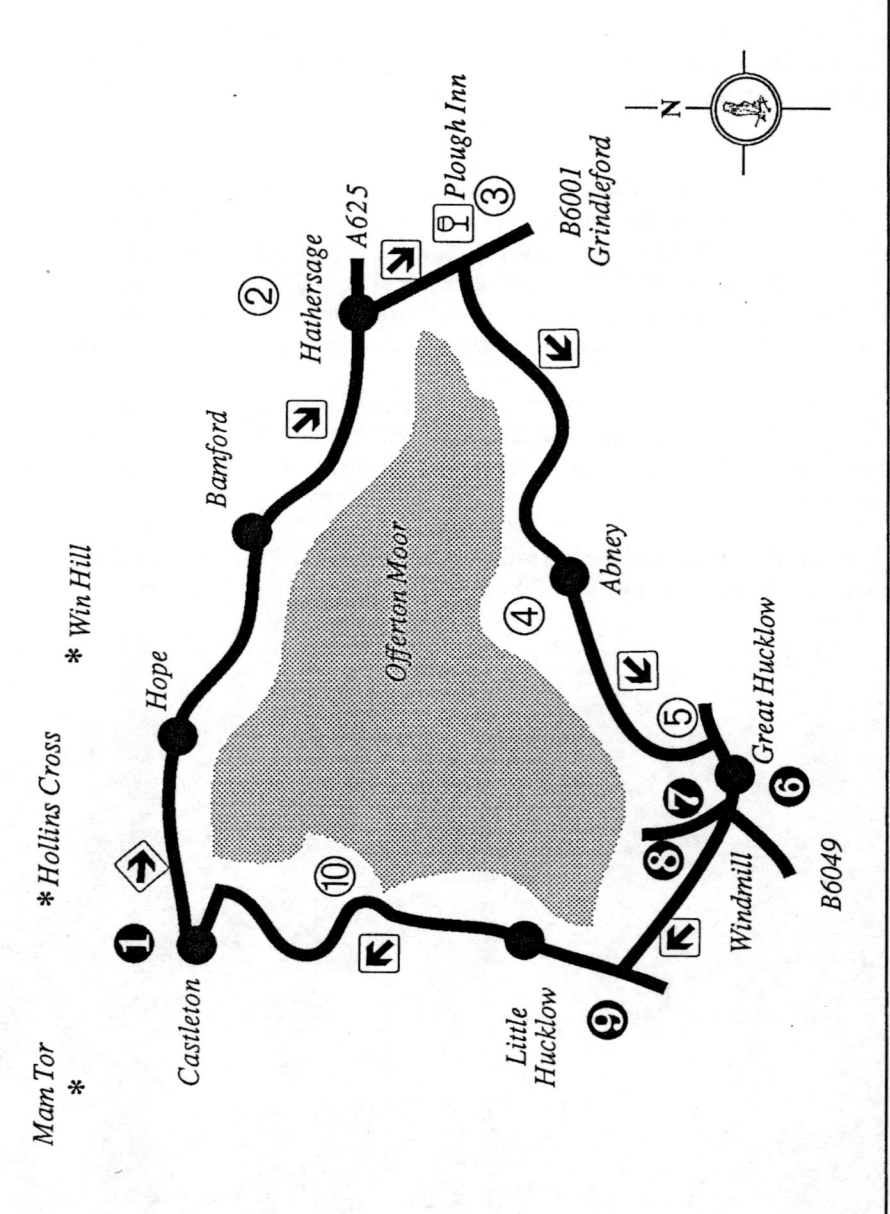

CASTLETON (B) - 18 MILES

Freewheel into Castleton, enjoying gorgeous views of Win Hill and Hollins Cross against the backdrop of Kinder Scout.

1. From Castleton, take the A625 into Hope, Bamford and Hathersage.

2 At Hathersage turn right on the B6001 signed Bakewell.

3 At the Plough Inn turn right, signed Abney.

4 Through Abney, the road forks, you can take either one.

5. At the acute 'T' junction turn right (no sign) to Great Hucklow 1/2 mile.

6 Through Great Hucklow, and past the Queen Anne on the left.

7 Right signed Bradwell 2 1/2 miles.

8 Immediately left, then forward, signed Windmill.

9 Right at the wider road (no sign). Then follow the Castleton signs.

10 Follow the signs back to the start, entering Castleton via Back Street. (This is a steep decent, with lovely views) turning left on the main road for the centre.

Winter view of Mam Tor showing the Iron age ditch around its summit.

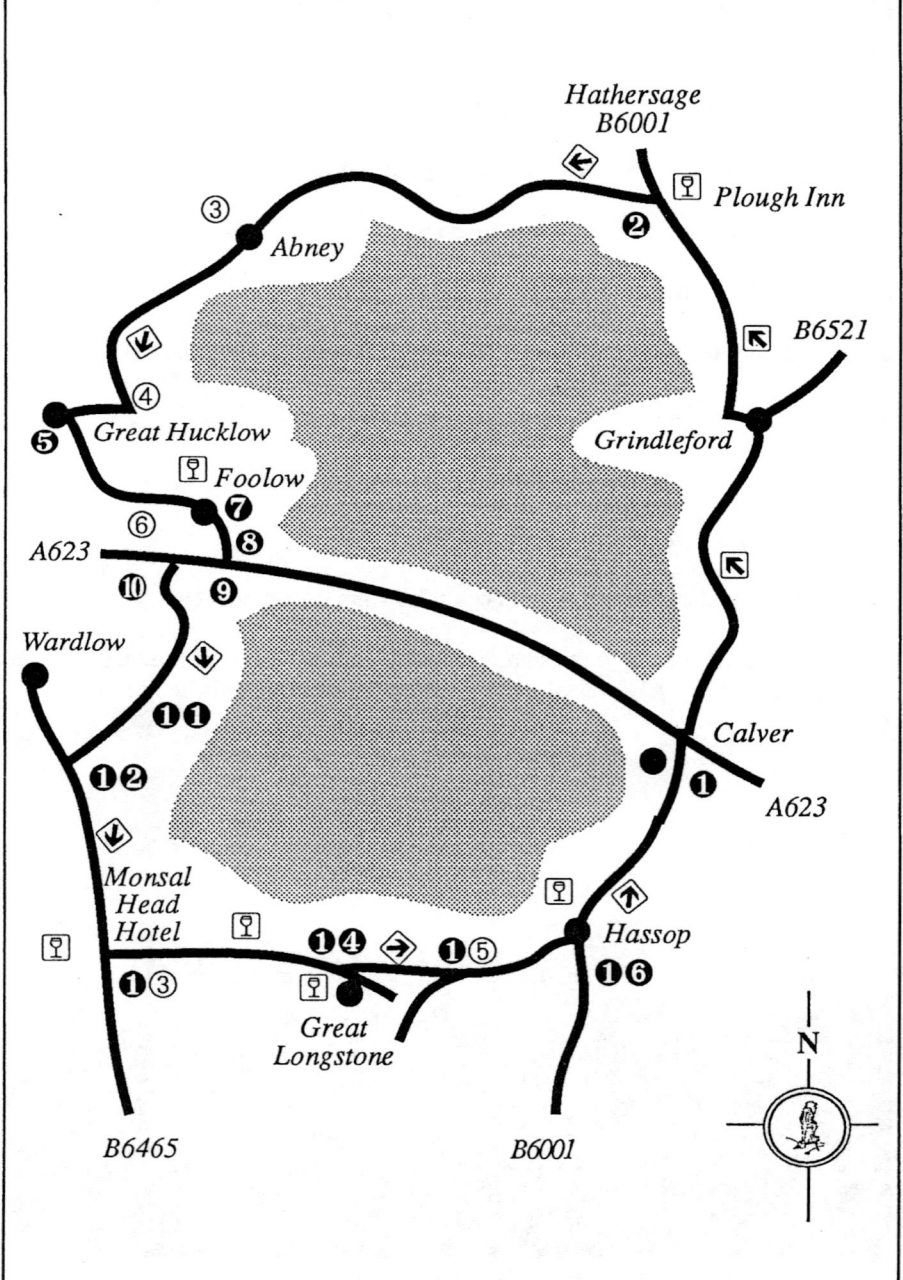

CALVER (C) - 20 MILES

Enjoy the bluebell woods on the way to Abney, (late May, early June) followed by an easy ride to Monsal Head and the attractive village of Great Longstone.

1 From Calver traffic lights to Grindleford go on the B6001 follow the signs to Hathersage.

2 At the Plough Inn at Leadmill, just before Hathersage, take the minor road on the left opposite the Plough and cycle towards Abney.

3 Through Abney towards Great Hucklow.

4 Right at the acute 'T' junction, (no sign).

5 Left to Grindlow.

6 Left to Foolow at 'T' junction (no sign, road wider.)

7 Turn right opposite the Bulls Head to Wardlow.

8 Right to Wardlow.

9 Right on the main road.

10 First left to Cavendish Mill.

11 At the first Jcn bear right, keep right at the Longstone Edge turning, to the B6465.

12 At the B 6465 turn left signed Ashford, to the Monsal Head Hotel.

13 From Monsal Head at Little Longstone turn left to Great Longstone. (Past the Pack Horse Inn, and the Crispin Inn.)

14 Look for Church Lane on the left, (easily missed) and turn up it.

15 Follow the signs to Hassop.

16 Left on the B6001 back to Calver.

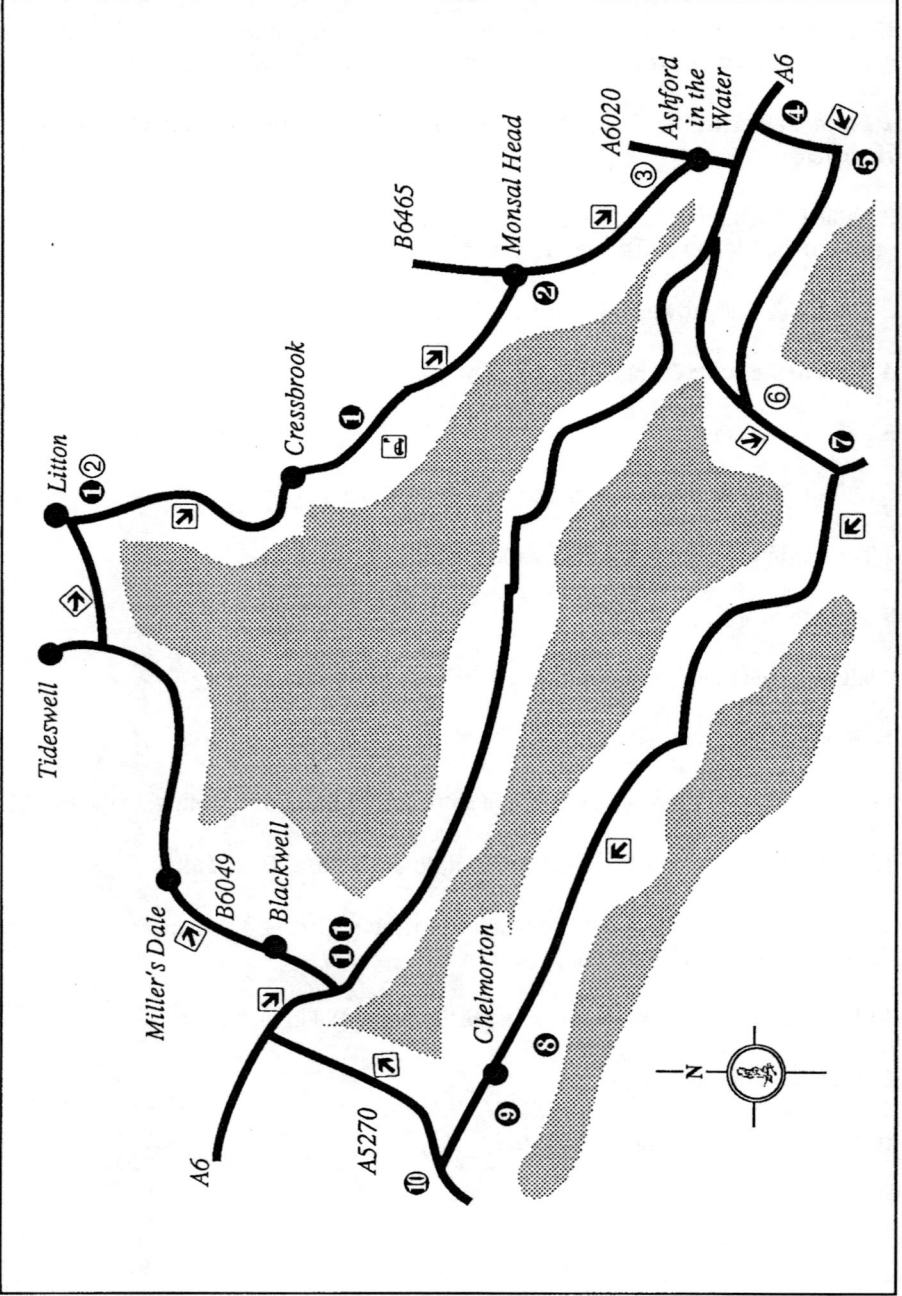

MONSAL HEAD (D) - 21 MILES.

Features :- The downhill run from Cressbrook to the finish. The village of Litton and the Monsal Head Hotel.

[P icon]. At the side of the river Wye, south of Cressbrook, near the Monsal Head hotel. map ref. 176723

1 From the car park, cycle south west with the river and the trail on your right up a steep hill, to the Monsal Head Hotel.

2 Right on B6465 signed Ashford.

3 As you enter Ashford turn left, right and left signed Bakewell on the A6.

4 First right signed Monyash 5 miles. (Sign for caravan site)

5 Right at T junction (not signed) (says Tideswell on stone marker) past Dirtlow Farm on the left.

6 Left at the wider road, and continue on this road to the top of the hill where you turn right at the 'T' junction. (No right arm on sign post.)

7 Right to Chelmorton 4 Miles and follow the Chelmorton signs.

8 At the Chelmorton boundary sign, immediately turn right

9 Left at the 'T' junction and first right along a narrow lane, just past a house called *SUNNY BANK 1908*. Adjacent to the old school. (Easily missed)

10 Right at 'T' junction (A5270) then right on the A6 signed Matlock.

11 Left B6049 signed Tideswell. Just before the Tideswell boundary sign, turn right following the signs to Litton.

12 In Litton right to Cressbrook and Millers Dale, turning left at the river and back to the start.

Route E - PARSLEY HAY - 14 MILES

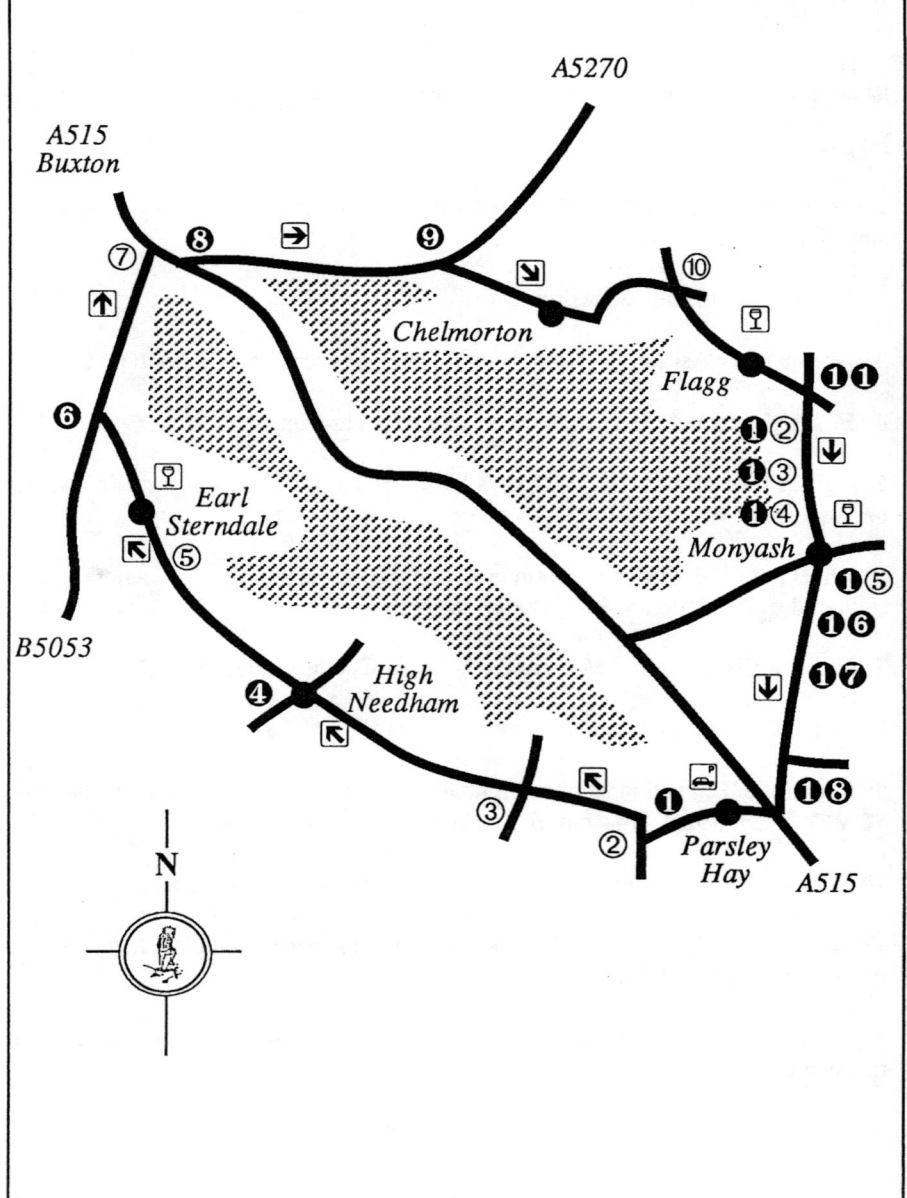

A5270

A515
Buxton

Chelmorton

Flagg

Monyash

Earl
Sterndale

High
Needham

B5053

Parsley
Hay

A515

N

PARSLEY HAY (E) - 14 MILES

Both this and the previous run, touch on Chelmorton, which is said to be the highest village in Derbyshire, having the highest church in England, with architecture dating from the 14th century. As none of the main roads go through Chelmorton, it must have the first by-pass ever built.

1   Exit the car park at Parsley Hay, turn right on the road, and go under the bridge.

2   Right, signed Pilsbury 2 1/4 miles.

3   Straight forward, signed Crowdecote.

4   Straight forward, signed Earl Sterndale 1 3/4 miles.

5   Right into the village of Earl Sterndale and past the Quiet Woman on the left.

6   Right B5053 signed Buxton.

7   Right A515 signed Ashbourne.

8   Left A5270 signed Bakewell 9 miles.

9   Right, signed Chelmorton.

10   Right signed Flagg 3/4 mile, and straight forward in Flagg, till you get to the Plough on the left.

11   Right fork to Monyash, 1 1/2 miles.

12   Right to Monyash 3/4 mile.

13   Into Monyash.

14   Straight forward, signed Monyash.

15   Across the B5055 signed Newhaven 4 miles, straight forward on Rakes Road. (Toilets on left)

16   Bear right to Newhaven 4 miles.

17   Straight forward signed Newhaven.

18   Left signed Newhaven 2 1/2 miles then immediately right and right again to the start.

Route F - BAKEWELL - 16 1/2 MILES

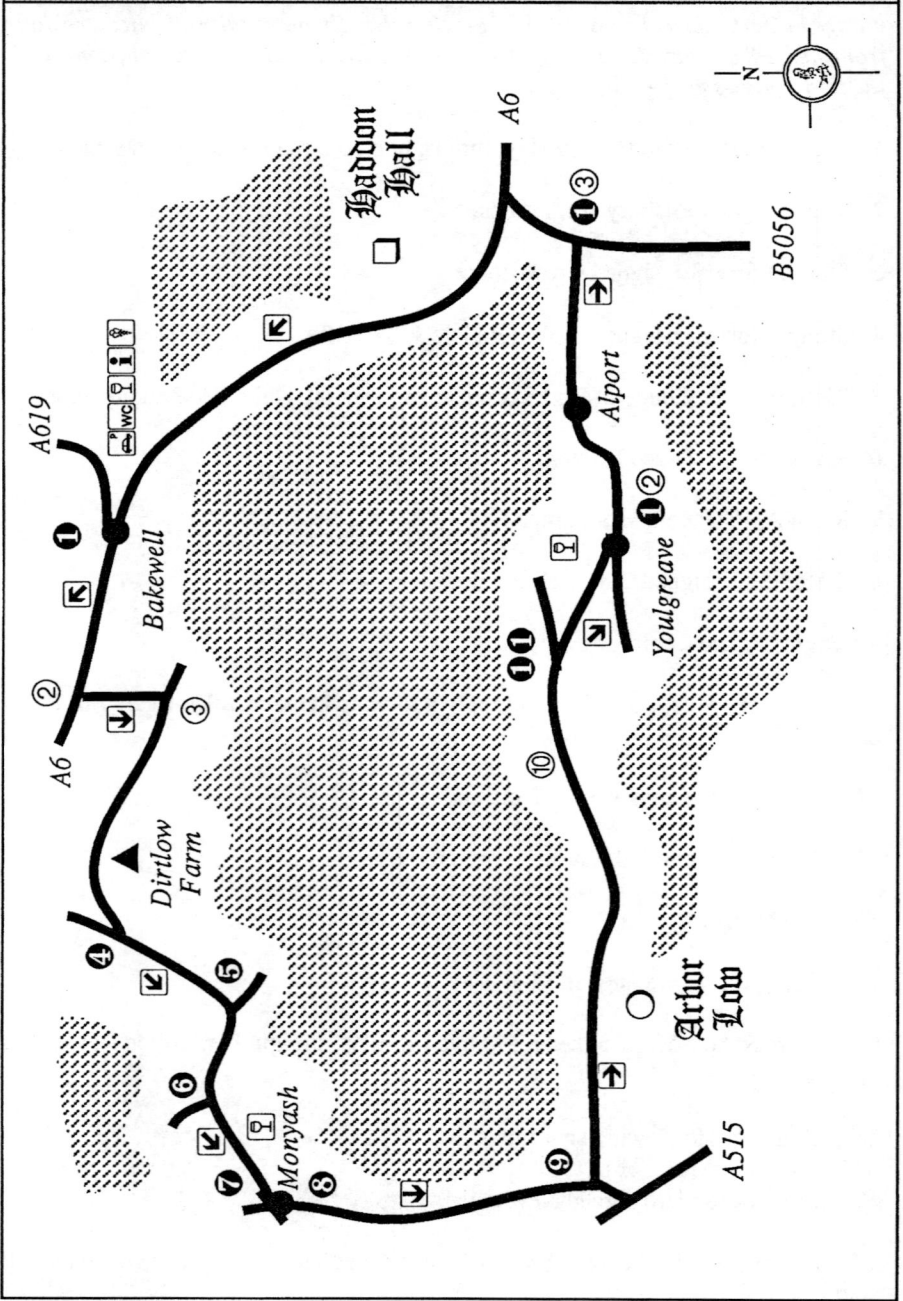

BAKEWELL (F) - 16 1/2 MILES

Points of interest - Monyash, and Youlgreave. this route brings you to Parsley Hay and if you take the northern route from Bakewell to Monyash, it is flatter and more pleasant than the B5056.

 Park in the Bakewell car parks, near the river and the market.

1   From the roundabout at Bakewell take the A6 to Buxton.

2   Left, signed Over Haddon. (sign for caravan site)

3   Right at T junction. (Not signed) Past Dirtlow Farm on the left.

4   Bear left at the wider road, and continue on this road to the top of the hill.

5   Right at T junction. (No right arm on sign-post)

6   Bear left at bend, signed Ashford and Monyash.

7   Left, signed Monyash.

8   Straight across B5055, signed Newhaven (Rakes road)

9   Bear right uphill to Youlgreave.

10   Left to Youlgreave. (Before reaching the main road.)

11   Keep bearing left (past a works) until you reach a lay-by and a clearway road sign where you turn right signed 'picnic site' (Moor Lane car park)

12   At Youlgreave, left in the village, onto the main road, and through Alport.

13   Left on the B5065. Then left on the A6 and back to Bakewell.

Route G - MONSAL TRAIL - 12 MILES

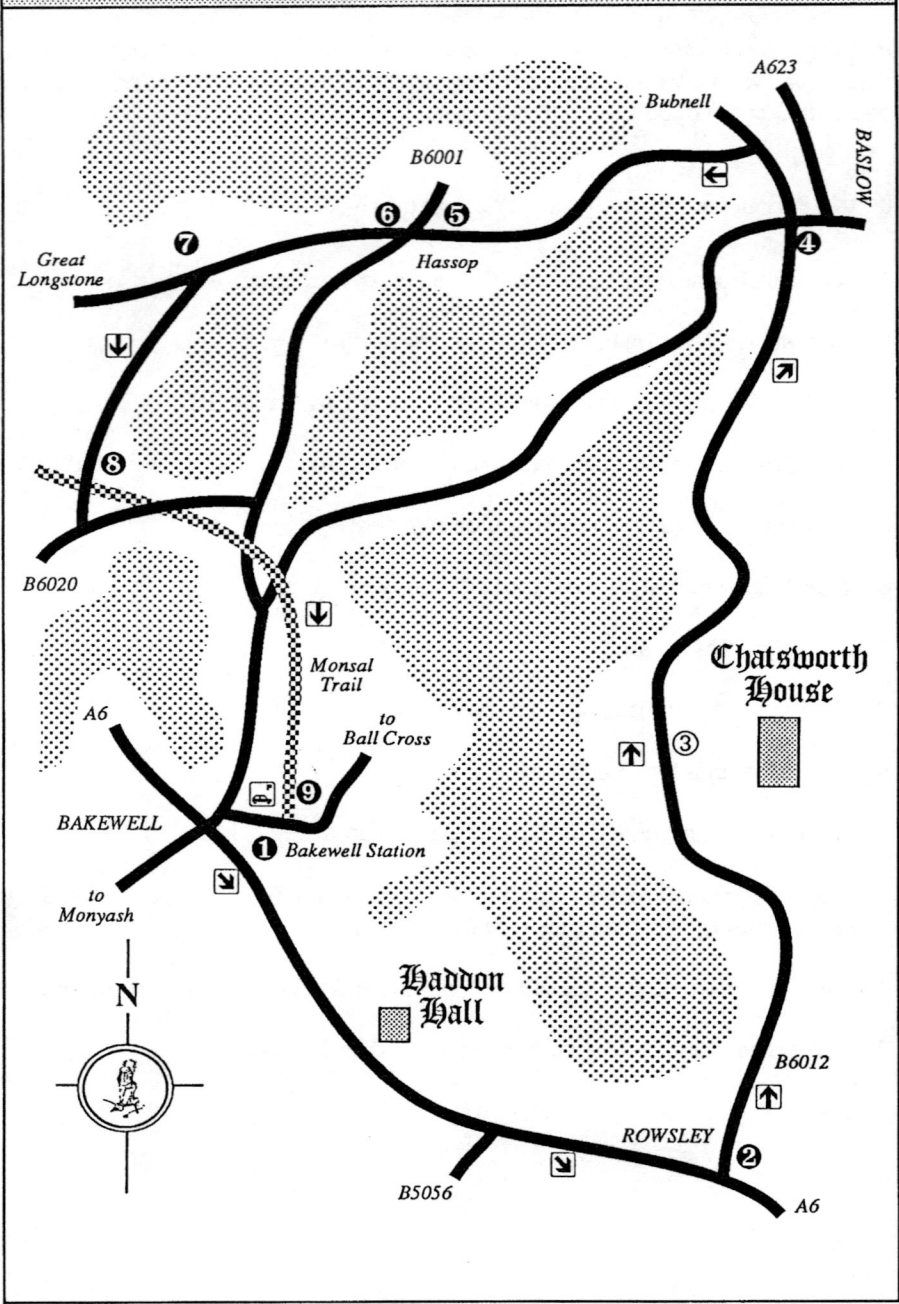

MONSAL TRAIL (G) - 12 MILES.

Undulating in parts, going through the grounds of Chatsworth house, passing Haddon Hall on the A6, and taking in part of the Monsal Trail. Generally fast, flat and pretty.

1   From Bakewell station which is the end of the Monsal trail, go down the hill to Bakewell and turn left on the A6 following the Matlock signs. Past Haddon Hall, the Peacock Hotel and the Grouse and Claret.

2   Left signed Baslow on the B6012. Over the narrow humped back bridge and through Chatsworth following the signs to Baslow.

3   From Chatsworth, head north on the B6012 towards Baslow.

4   Just before the bridge at Baslow turn left, signed Bubnell (this turn is easily missed, Bakewell road), then first left again up Wheatlands Lane, with a sign saying unsuitable for coaches.

5   At the end, turn left, on the B6001 signed Bakewell and past the Eyre Arms on the right.

6   Just past the Eyre Arms turn right signed Rowland and Great Longstone, with Hassop Hall on the left. (Looks as though you are going straight forward).

7   Take the first left, (no signpost) down Long Greave Lane, Rowland.

8   At the bottom of the hill is a bridge, this is the Monsal trail, there is easy access via a path on the left just before the bridge.

9   Turn left on the trail, (south east) back to Bakewell station.

Route H - HULME END - 15 MILES

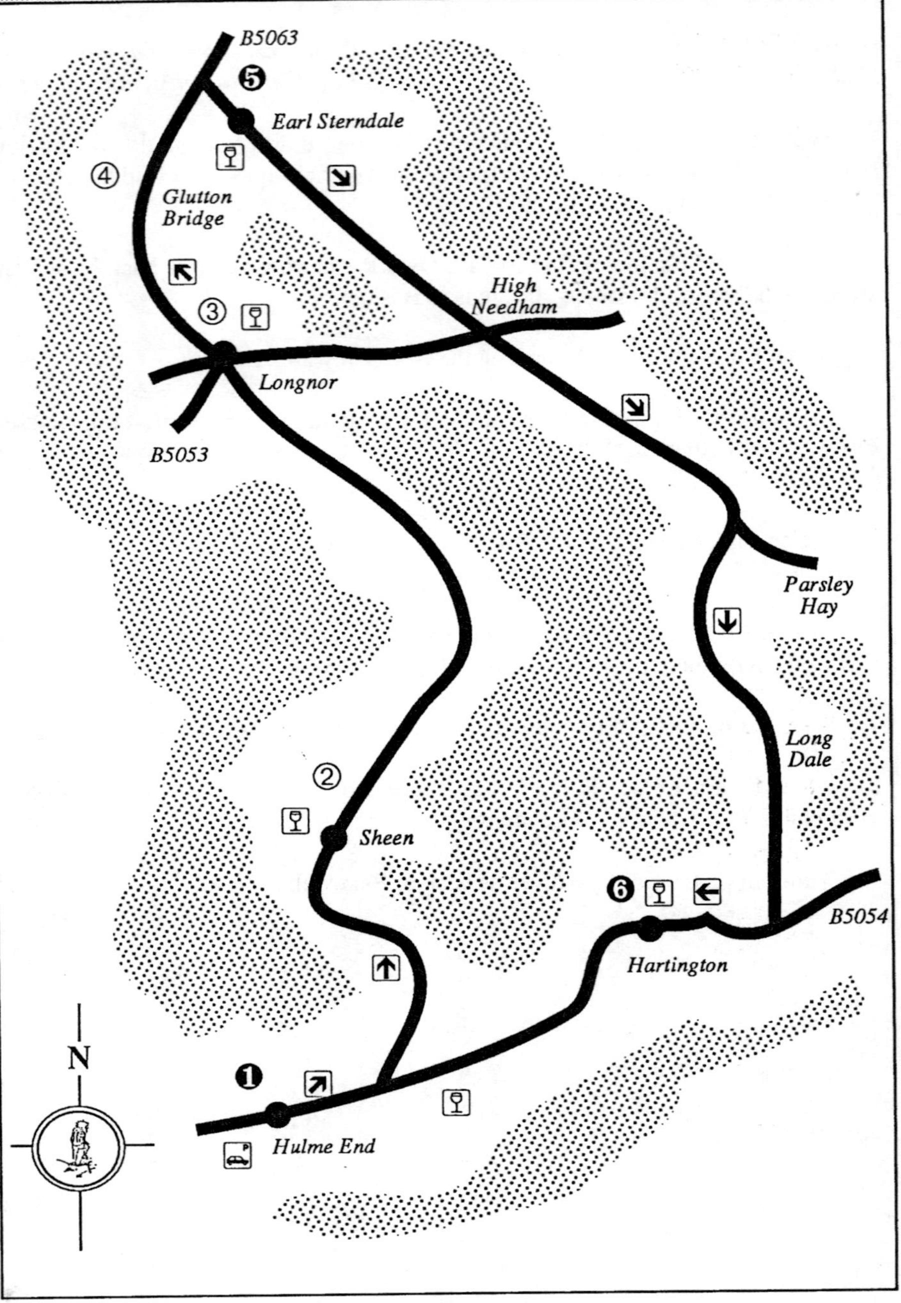

B5063

❺ Earl Sterndale

④ Glutton Bridge

③ Longnor

High Needham

B5053

Parsley Hay

Long Dale

② Sheen

❻ Hartington

B5054

❶

Hulme End

N

22

HULME END (H) - 15 MILES.

Seeing Crowdecote, nestling in the upper reaches of the Dove valley, bathed in sunlight, is an experience not to be missed.

1 From the car park at Hulme End, turn right on the B5054 and take the second left signed Sheen, and follow the signs to Longnor.

2 Past the Staffordshire Knott on the left and into Longnor.

3 From Longnor, take the B5053 uphill, past the Horseshoe Inn on the left corner, then the Fire Station (also on the left) towards Earl Sterndale.

4 Over Glutton Bridge, into Glutton.

5 Right to Earl Sterndale, past the Quiet Woman on the right, go forward, then soon left following the signs to Hartington.

6 From Hartington turn right on the B5054 back to Hulme End.

The Square, Hartington.

Route I - FRIDEN (Newhaven) - 24 MILES

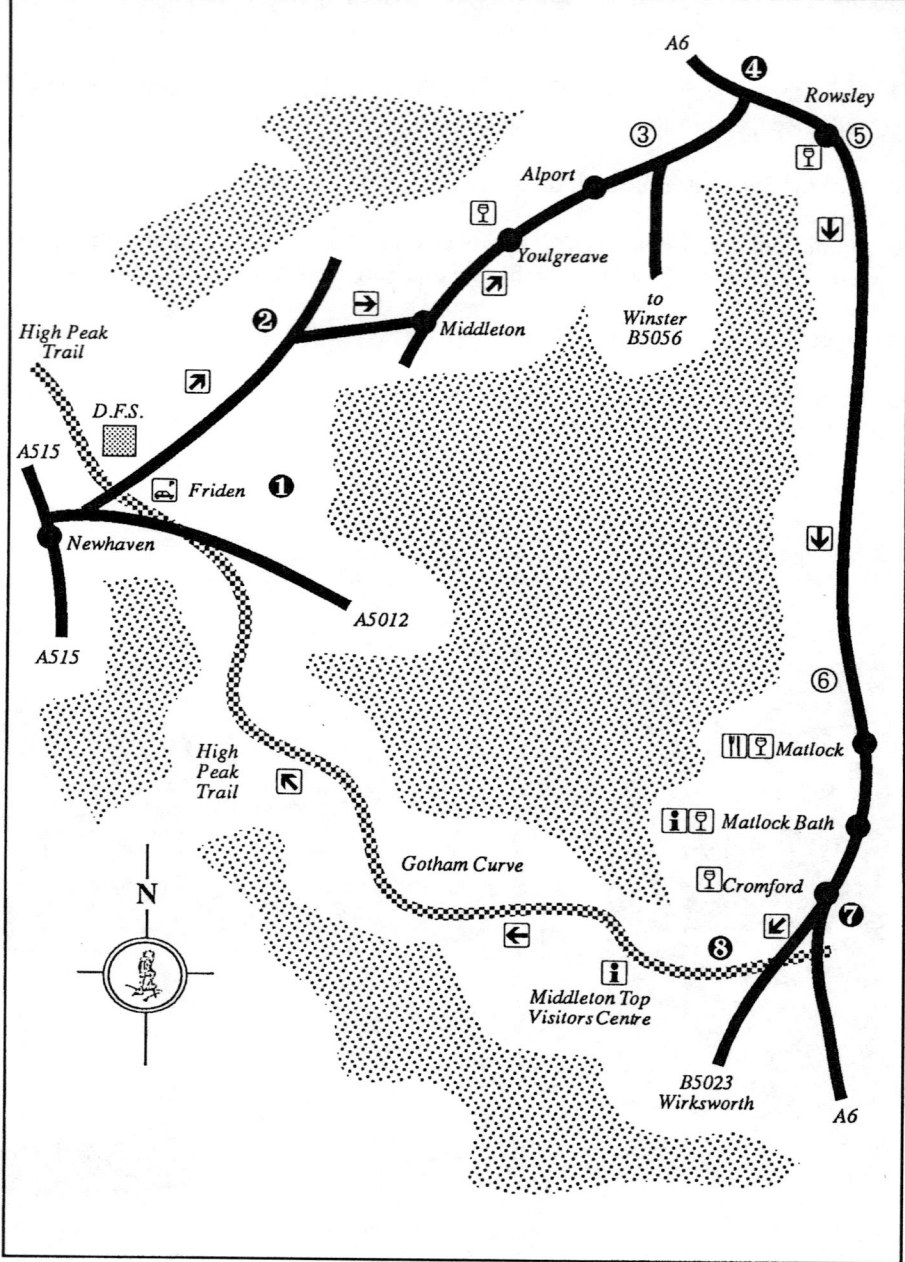

FRIDEN (Newhaven) (I) - 24 MILES

A fast flat ride, apart from a steep hill at Cromford, and another on the High Peak Trail.

1   From the car park at Friden (just north of Newhaven) turn right opposite the offices of D.F.S. and go under the bridge.

2   Right to Middleton one mile, and follow the signs to Youlgreave.

3   Left on the B5056 signed Bakewell.

4   Right on the A6 signed Matlock.

5   Through Rowsley and follow the signs to Matlock.

6   Into Matlock, turning right, following A6 Derby sign, and over the river bridge, then turn left.

7   At the traffic lights at Cromford, turn right on the A5012, then go straight forward, on the Wirksworth road, up Cromford hill. This brings you to Black Rocks. The High Peak Trail is signed, turn right on the trail crossing Cromford Hill on the viaduct.

8   Back to Friden on the High Peak Trail.

Black Rocks - a popular rock climbing area and vantage point.

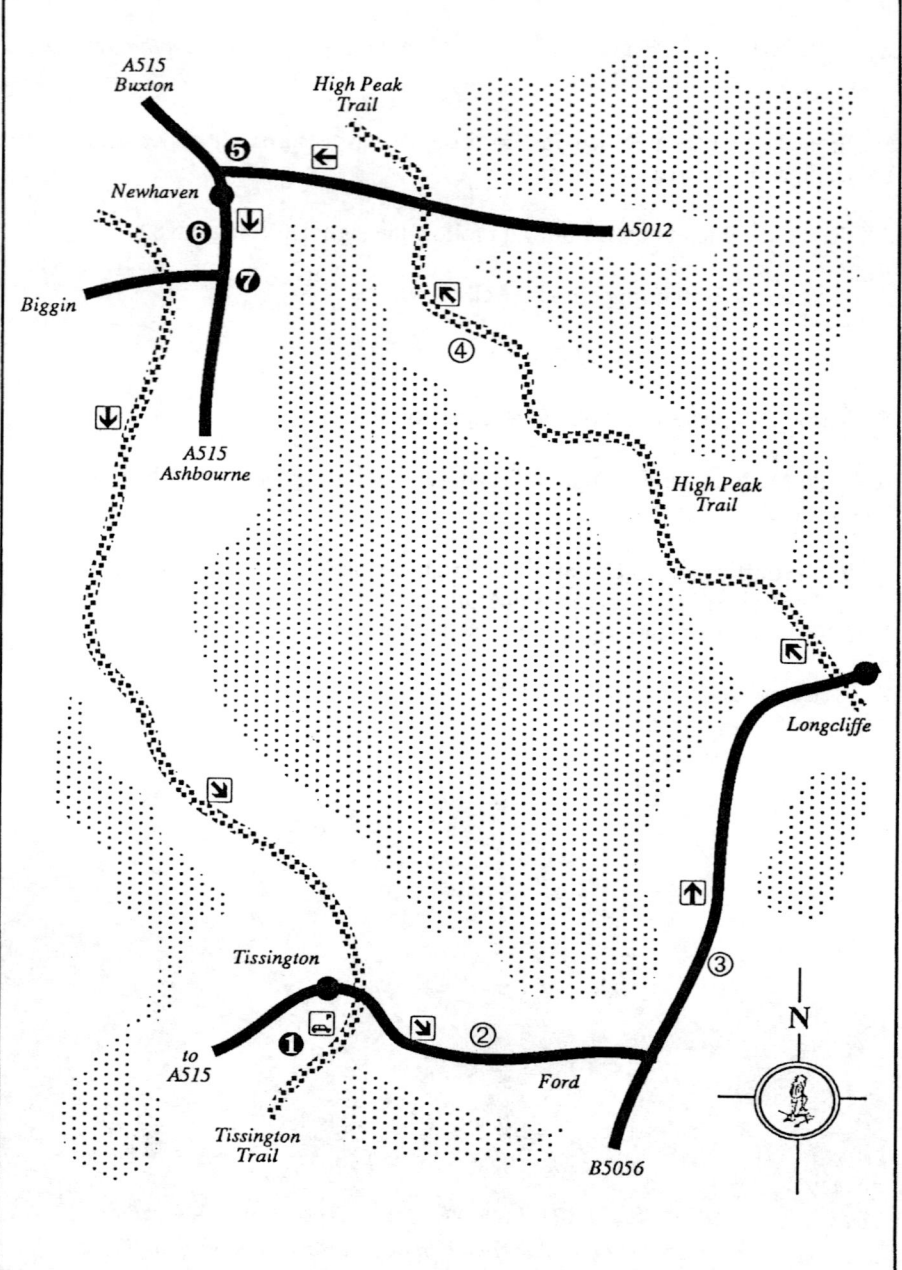

TISSINGTON (J) - 15 MILES.

Another fast flat run. The view from Tissington to the ford seems different from the rest of the Peak District, a pleasant change and an easy ride.

1 From the car park at Tissington on the trail (the name is over the toilet block.) go over the bridge, turning right, past a row of houses on the left, dated 1840. (travelling east.)

2 Straight forward till you get to a ford, and turn left on the Bakewell Rd.

3 Stay on the Bakewell road, and at the top of an incline, there is a house painted white on the right, (the old railway station) near to a viaduct, this is the High Peak Trail. Make your way on to the trail through a gap in the wall and turn left relative to the road you have just come up. (west)

4 At the Picnic site at Minninglow, bear right keeping on the cycle trail till you get to the A5012 and turn left. (This is the first road you come to.) (Alternatively, carry on to Parsley Hay, turning left on the Tissington trail and back to the start at Tissington. This adds 4 miles.)

5 Left again on the A515.

6 Past the dilapidated New Haven Hotel on the right.

7 First right, signed Biggin. The Tissington trail crosses this road, there is easy access through a gate on the right. Turn left on the trail relative to the road you have just come on and head south back to Tissington.

Tissington Hall.

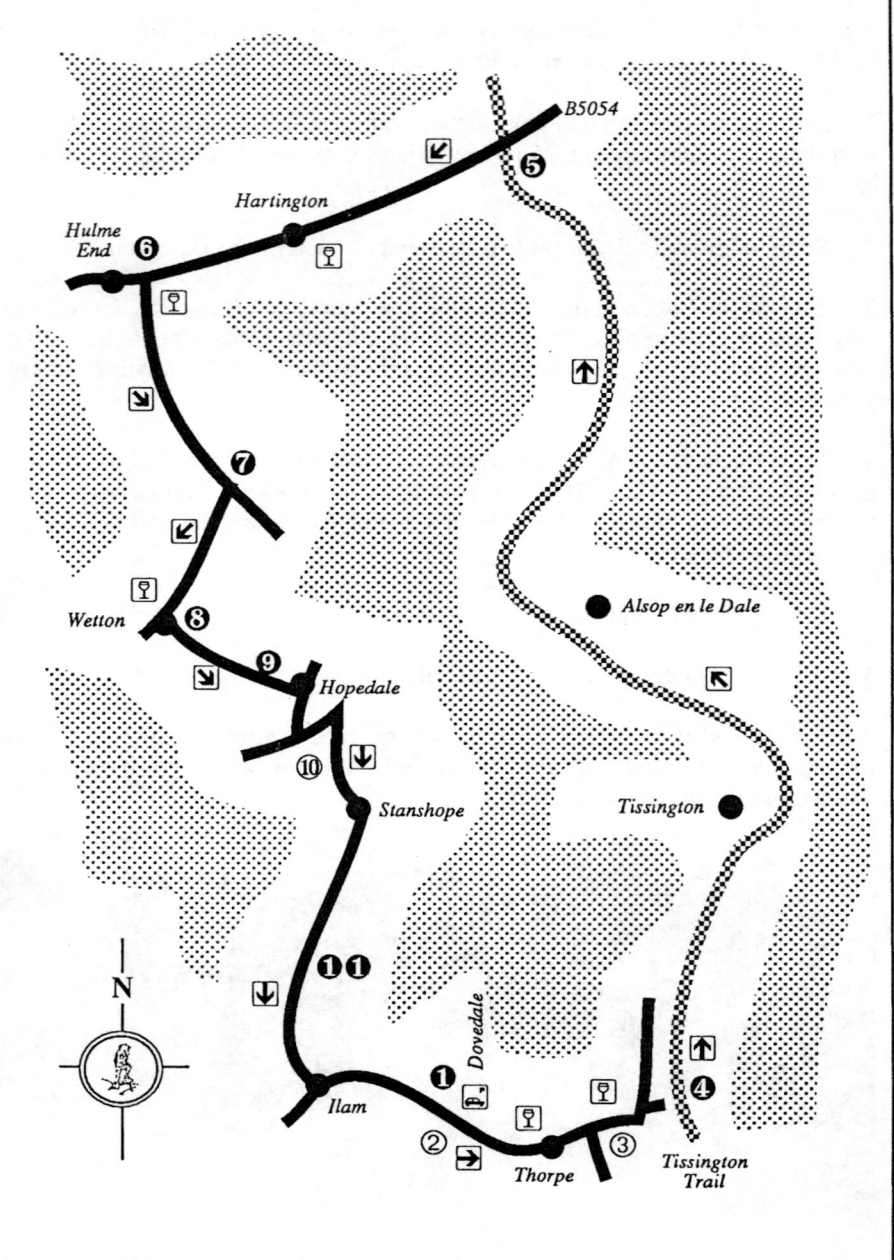

DOVEDALE (K) - 23 MILES.

Visit the Ilam village church and. the grounds of the Hall (now a Youth Hostel) with of course beautiful Dovedale and the stepping stones.

1   From the car park at Dovedale, turn left out of the car park and left again.

2   Over two cattle grids, and into Thorpe, (Tissington 2 miles) passing the Peveril of the Peak Hotel on the left.

3   At the Dog and Partridge, second left (which looks straight forward,) signed Tissington 1 1/2 miles, and in a few yards turn right, down a lane, (following a car parking sign) onto the Tissington trail.

4   Left on the trail (NE) and a long stretch to Hartington Signal box.

5   Down hill from the car park at the Hartington Signal Box, and turn left on the B5054 to Hulme End.

6   Turn left at the Manifold Valley Hotel.

7   Forward, signed Wetton 2 3/4 miles and follow the signs to Wetton.

8   At the "Ye Olde Royal Oak" turn left, signed Ilam 3 3/4 miles. (Dovedale)

9   Left again, also signed Ilam 3 3/4 miles. (Dovedale)

10   Right, signed Dovedale 4 miles, and in a little while into Stanshope.

11   Forward into Ilam 1/4 mile, then left to Dovedale 3/4 mile and back to the start.

Route L - MANIFOLD WAY - 22 MILES

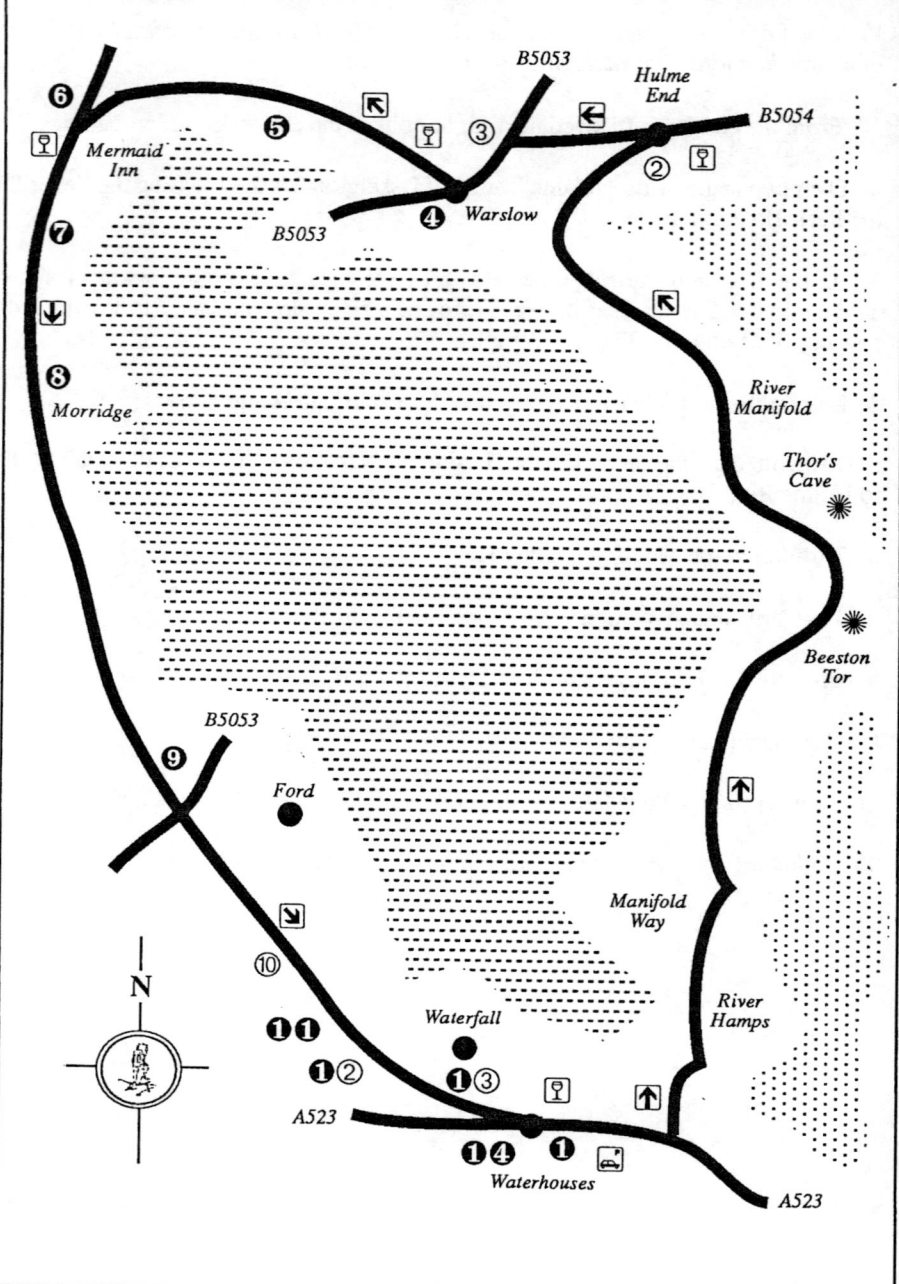

MANIFOLD WAY (L) - 22 MILES.

The view west to the Roaches is breathtaking, followed by an easy downhill ride back along the Morridge.

🅿️ - On the A523 near Waterhouses is a car park, near the cycle hire at the start of the Manifold way.

1 Along the Manifold Way to the Hulme End car park. The route of the Manifold Way can be confusing. At the first road junction (Weags bridge) go straight forward (obvious). At the second road junction (road open to traffic) take the first left. At the third road junction, (shallow ford) the second left, and left before the bridge. Through the tunnel, straight forward, and at the next road junction also straight forward (obvious) so to the Hulme End car park.

2 At the Hulme end car park turn left on the B5064 (West).

3 Left on the B5053 into Warslow.

4 First right, signed Newtown, going past the Greyhound Inn on the right.

6 Follow the signs for Leek.

7 At the Mermaid Inn turn left.

8 At the sign saying 'ALTERNATIVE ROUTE FOR LORRIES' turn left.

9 Keep going straight forward, along the Morridge following signs for Bottom Houses, and Ford (Be careful to give way at a main road).

10 Straight forward, at the Ford/New Street intersection.

11 Past the sign 'ROAD LIABLE TO FLOODING' and over the bridge.

12 At the end, turn left, and in twenty yards turn right, down a rough track.

13 At the end of Cross Lane turn right.

14 Turn left on the A52 by 'The George'.

15 Into Waterhouses, and back to the start.

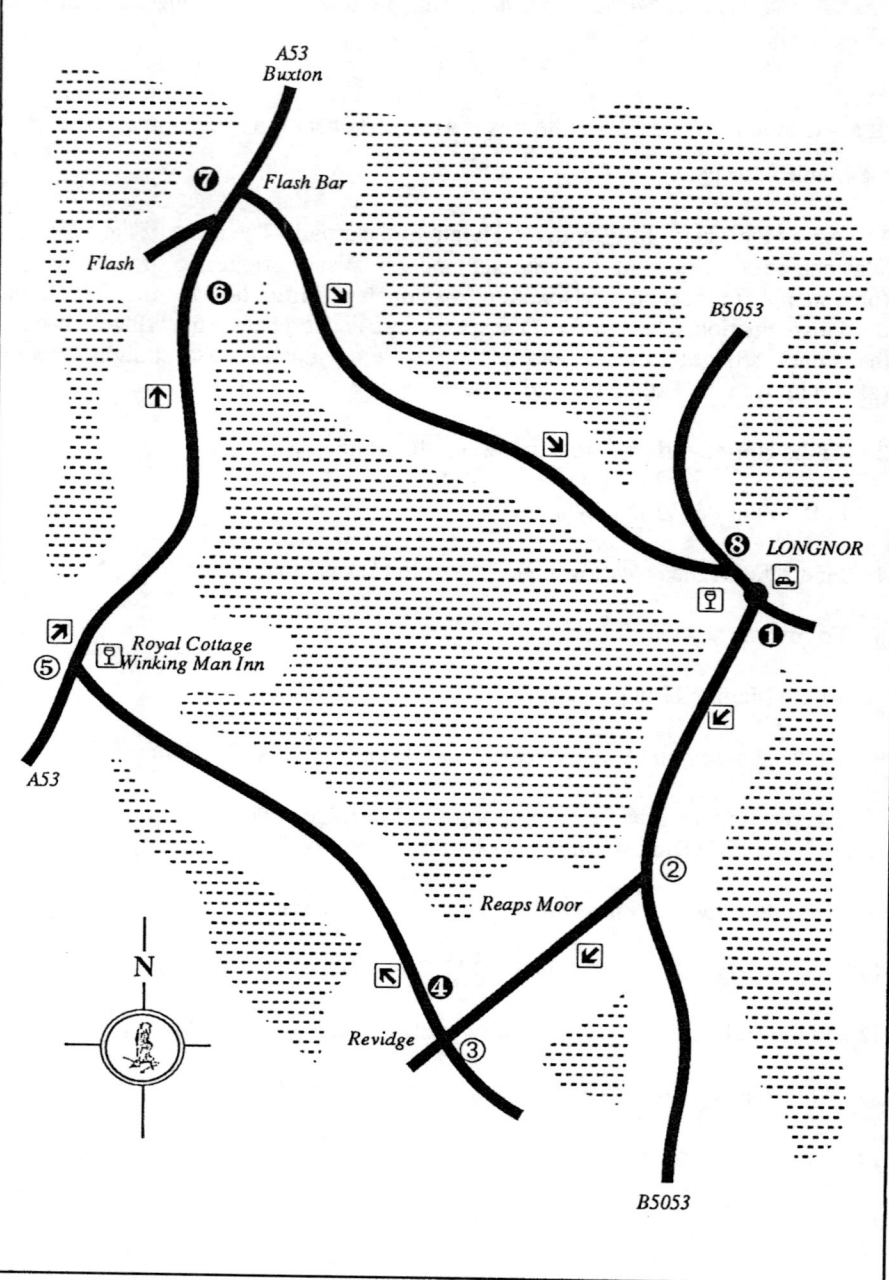

LONGNOR (M) - 15 MILES.

More views of the Roaches, The road from Flash Bar Stores is on a spur, with good views of the moors on either side, as you freewheel down info Longnor. (There can be dangerous cross winds on the A53, a calm day would be advisable.)

1   From Longnor, go downhill on the B5053. signed Warslow 4 miles.

2   Take the second right, signed Reapsmoor 1 mile, and keep going straight forward.

3   Right, signed Leek 6 1/4 miles.

4   Follow signs for Royal Cottage. (Royal cottage is the pub, now called Winking Man)

5   Right on the A53 signed Buxton 7 miles. Winking Man on the corner.

6   Past the sign for the New Inn.

7   Right at Flash Bar stores signed Longnor 5 miles. (Keep on this road).

8   Right at the bottom of the hill on the B5053 and you are back in Longnor.

The Roaches one fine January day, after a sprinkling of snow.

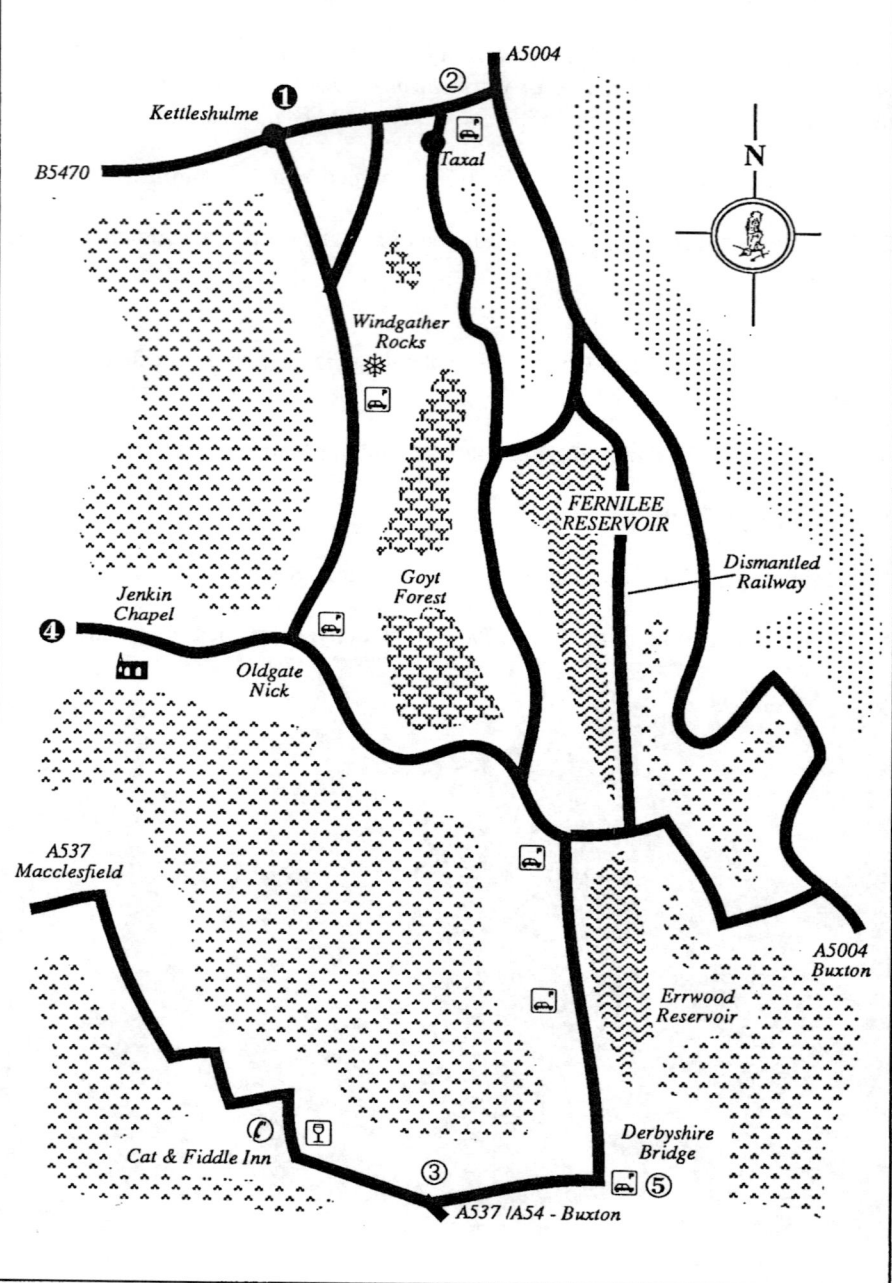

Route N - GOYT VALLEY

Kettleshulme

B5470

A5004

Taxal

Windgather Rocks

N

Jenkin Chapel

Oldgate Nick

Goyt Forest

FERNILEE RESERVOIR

Dismantled Railway

A537 Macclesfield

A5004 Buxton

Errwood Reservoir

Cat & Fiddle Inn

Derbyshire Bridge

A537 /A54 - Buxton

GOYT VALLEY (N).

There are several ways into and out of the Goyt Valley.

1   From Kettleshulme, a lovely downhill ride, to Derbyshire Bridge showing all the glories of the valley.

2   From the northern end of Errwood reservoir, near the car park go through the woods, onto a forest trail with limestone chippings, which when settled will make a good cycle path through to Taxal, then back via the A5002 to the traffic lights, turning right on the A5004 and back to Errwood turning right into the main access road to the northern end of Errwood reservoir.

3   From the south, the A537 to Errwood Reservoir is the flattest road and makes a linear route similar to Derwent Valley.

4   The road via. Jenkin Chapel, is not recommended as it is far too steep.

5   For an easy circular tour; start from Derbyshire Bridge, and take the A54 into Buxton, then the A5004, turning left to the top of Errwood reservoir and back to Derbyshire Bridge.

NOTE - A one way traffic system operates between Errwood reservoir and Derbyshire Bridge, ie traffic flows north to south.

Jenkin Chapel.

35

THE BIG ONE - 80 MILES AROUND THE PEAK DISTRICT

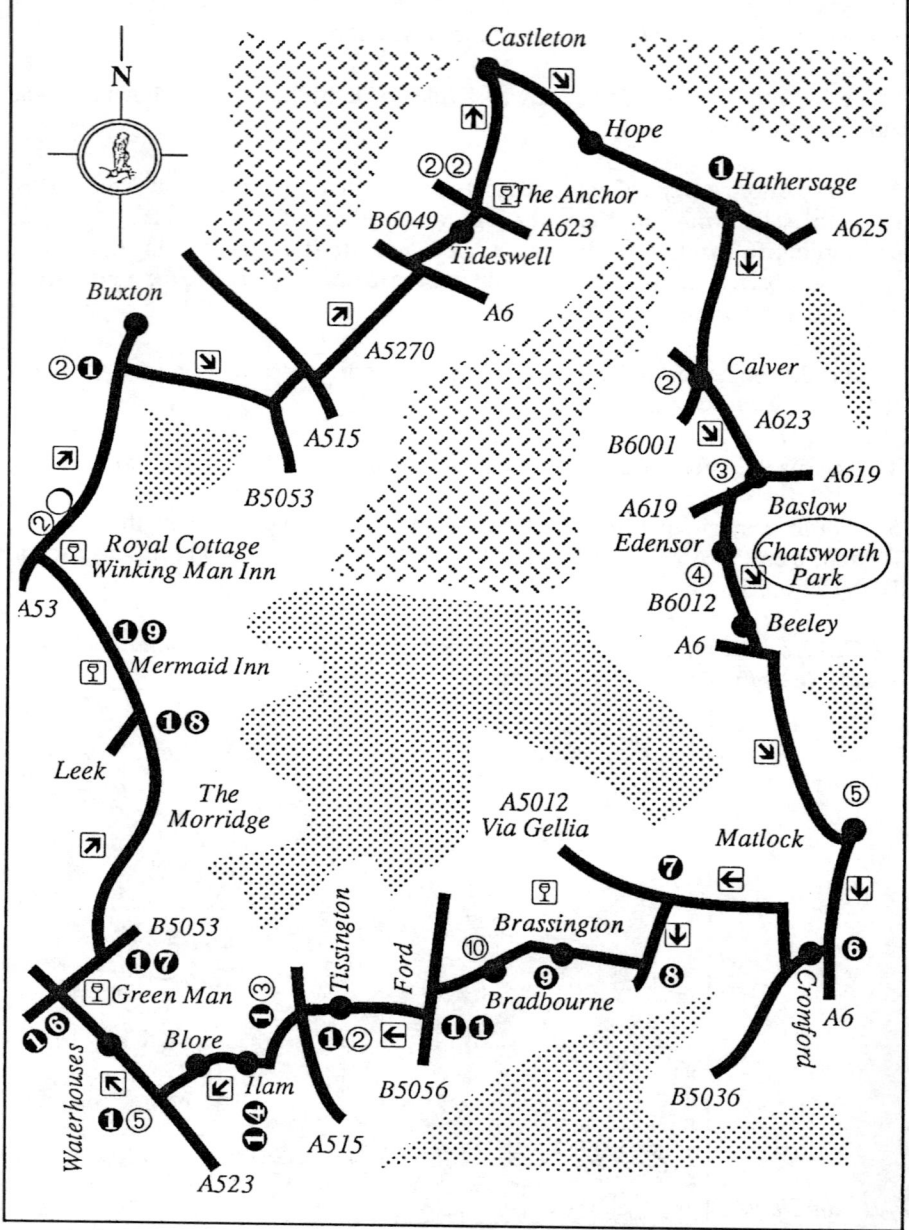

THE BIG ONE - 80 MILES.

Start anywhere. Suggest.

1 From Hathersage take the B6001 signed Bakewell. Right at Grindleford (B6001 Bakewell).

2 Calver Left A623 signed Chesterfield.

3 Baslow Right A619 signed Bakewell then straight on B6012 signed Chatsworth.

4 Through Chatsworth following the A6 to Matlock.

5 At Matlock, keep on the A6 and follow Derby signs.

6 At Cromford traffic lights, Right B5036 signed Wirksworth, Right A5012 signed Newhaven (Via Gellia).

7 Left B5023 signed Middleton, immediately bear right signed Ryder Point.

8 Right under the viaduct signed Brassington 2 miles.

9 At Brassington, turn right to Bradbourne by the village stores.

10 At Bradbourne follow the signs to Fenny Bentley.

11 Left B5056 signed Fenny Bentley and first right through a ford. (Don't miss this).

12 Straight forward, over the A515 signed Dovedale.

13 At the Dog and Partridge, straight forward to Thorpe.

14 Follow signs to Dovedale. At the monument in Ilam turn left over the bridge signed Blore 1 mile.

15 Follow the Leek signposts turning Right A523, and go through Waterhouses and Winkhill.

16 At the Green Man, Right B5053 signed Longnor.

17 First Left on the Morridge signed Bradnop 2 3/4 miles.

18 Right at the T Jcn (sign saying alternative route for lorries).

19 Past the Mermaid on the left, and follow the signs to the Royal Cottage.

20 Right at the Winking Man to Buxton.

21 Right (A515) signed Ashbourne (Harpur Hill) and follow the Ashbourne signs.

Left B5053.
Right A515.
Left A5270 Bakewell Road.
Right A6 signed Matlock.
Left B6049 to Tideswell.

22 Across A623 Left and immediately Left in front of the Anchor, to Castleton.

(Alternatively take the Bradwell B6049 road, which is easier and quicker).

Keep right through Castleton, then Right on the A625 at Castleton, through Hope and back to the start at Hathersage.

A popular Derbyshire custom - Well Dressing at Wirksworth.

DATE	ROUTE	COMMENTS

SOME OTHER SUGGESTIONS
- ROUTES, CHALLENGES AND QUICKIE'S -

CURBAR to CRICH.

1.   From the car park at CURBAR, turn left uphill (east) and go straight across the A621 and the B6050.

2   After the B6050 in a few yards bear left, then first right signed Eastmoor.

3   Straight across A619 signed Beeley, and follow signs to Darley Dale, turning left at T junction (no sign) then follow the signs to Matlock.

4   At the A632 left & first right signed Woolley 3 miles, then right signed Matlock avoiding steep hill.

5   Keep going straight forward, across B6014 signed Lee. Across A615 along High Lane.

6   Right then left signed CRICH.

CRICH to CURBAR.

1   From CRICH, go along Plaistow Green Rd turning right on High Lane following the Tansley signs.

2   At Lickpenny Lane. follow the Ashover 2 1/2 mile sign.

3   Straight across A615 & B6014 signed Kelstedge.

4   At the A632 left & immediately right signed Darley Dale 4 miles, keep straight forward to B5057.

5   At the B5057 straight across signed Beeley, across the next junction also signed Beeley, THEN 1st RIGHT (no sign) and second left following signs to Eastmoor which brings you to the A619.

6   Straight across A619 and first left signed Baslow then right and follow the signs back to CURBAR

A CHALLENGE -

From Glutton bridge, which is just north of Longnor on the B5053, is a telephone Kiosk, at the side of which is a minor road. It goes to Axe Edge, and is very steep, but beautiful. A lot cyclists use it. See how long it takes to get to the top and if you can get up without stopping.

Quickie 1.

Eyam is on a hill side, which usually means a climb. There is a triangle of minor roads just north of Eyam, with ample car parking. The road to Great Hucklow is flat and glorious in the atumn when the heather is out, with Eyam just down the road.

Quickie 2.

At Wildboarclough, south east of Macclesfield are a series of car parks. The road is flat at that point and very quiet, it is also part of the Cheshire Cycle Way.

Quickie 3

At Cromford is a flat minor road running parallel to the A6. It has the added attractions of the Arkwright Mill Museum, Model Railway Museum, Cromford Mill, the start of the High Peak Trail, (Black Rocks) the canal, and further on the home of Florence Nightingale with the National Tramway Museum at Crich, (steeper here) and of course joins up with the Crich to Curbar run on the previous page. A circular route could be made here by coming back on the A6.

Quickie 4

The Middlewood cycle way runs between Macclesfield and Marple, on a disused railway line for about 10 miles.

Quickie 5

Another flat road is from Hope to Edale through to Barber Booth. If you feel like a challenge you can continue on, then freewheel down Winnats Pass, through Castleton and back to Hope.

Quickie 6

From the car park at Fenny Bentley on the Tissington Trail (vehicle access is from Thorpe near the Dog and Partridge,) go north up the trail to Alsop en le Dale. Turn left on the A515 and in a few yards you will come to the New Holiday Inn on the left painted white. Just after that, on the right is a narrow road without a signpost, and a notice which says 'GATES, SINGLE TRACK ROAD'. Go along this road, through two gates, (picnic between the gates) and back to Thorpe. This is the easiest way round.

OTHER JOHN MERRILL BOOKS FROM
Happy Walking International Ltd.,

For a full list of titles - more than 300 - write for a free catalog to-

Happy Walking International Ltd.,
Unit 1,
Molyneux Business Park,
Whitworth Road,
Darley Dale,
Matlock,
Derbyshire.
DE4 2HJ

THE LITTLE JOHN CHALLENGE WALK
YORKSHIRE DALES CHALLENGE WALK
NORTH YORKSHIRE MOORS CHALLENGE WALK
LAKELAND CHALLENGE WALK
THE RUTLAND WATER CHALLENGE WALK
MALVERN HILLS CHALLENGE WALK
THE SALTER'S WAY
THE SNOWDON CHALLENGE
CHARNWOOD FOREST CHALLENGE WALK
THREE COUNTIES CHALLENGE WALK (Peak District).
CAL-DER-WENT WALK by Geoffrey Carr,
THE QUANTOCK WAY
BELVOIR WITCHES CHALLENGE WALK
THE CARNEDDAU CHALLENGE WALK

INSTRUCTION & RECORD -
HIKE TO BE FIT.....STROLLING WITH JOHN
THE JOHN MERRILL WALK RECORD BOOK

MULTIPLE DAY WALKS -
THE RIVERS'S WAY
PEAK DISTRICT: HIGH LEVEL ROUTE
PEAK DISTRICT MARATHONS
THE LIMEY WAY
THE PEAKLAND WAY
COMPO'S WAY by Alan Hiley

COAST WALKS & NATIONAL TRAILS -
ISLE OF WIGHT COAST PATH
PEMBROKESHIRE COAST PATH
THE CLEVELAND WAY
WALKING ANGELSEY'S COASTLINE.

CYCLING Compiled by Arnold Robinson.
CYCLING AROUND THE NORTH YORK MOORS .
CYCLING AROUND MATLOCK.
CYCLING AROUND LEICES & RUTLAND.
CYCLING AROUND CASTLETON & the Hope Valley.
CYCLING AROUND CHESTERFIELD.
CYCLING IN THE YORKSHIRE WOLDS
CYCLING AROUND BUXTON.
CYCLING AROUND LINCOLNSHIRE.

PEAK DISTRICT HISTORICAL GUIDES -
A to Z GUIDE OF THE PEAK DISTRICT
DERBYSHIRE INNS - an A to Z guide
HALLS AND CASTLES OF THE PEAK DISTRICT & DERBYSHIRE
TOURING THE PEAK DISTRICT & DERBYSHIRE BY CAR
DERBYSHIRE FOLKLORE
PUNISHMENT IN DERBYSHIRE
CUSTOMS OF THE PEAK DISTRICT & DERBYSHIRE
WINSTER - a souvenir guide
ARKWRIGHT OF CROMFORD
LEGENDS OF DERBYSHIRE
DERBYSHIRE FACTS & RECORDS
TALES FROM THE MINES by Geoffrey Carr
PEAK DISTRICT PLACE NAMES by Martin Spray

JOHN MERRILL'S MAJOR WALKS -
TURN RIGHT AT LAND'S END
WITH MUSTARD ON MY BACK
TURN RIGHT AT DEATH VALLEY
EMERALD COAST WALK

SKETCH BOOKS -
SKETCHES OF THE PEAK DISTRICT

COLOUR BOOK:-
THE PEAK DISTRICT.......something to remember her by.

OVERSEAS GUIDES -
HIKING IN NEW MEXICO - Vol I - The Sandia and Manzano Mountains.
Vol 2 - Hiking "Billy the Kid" Country. Vol 4 - N.W. area - " Hiking Indian Country."
"WALKING IN DRACULA COUNTRY" - Romania.

VISITOR GUIDES - MATLOCK . BAKEWELL. ASHBOURNE.

CYCLING GUIDES
by ARNOLD
ROBINSON.

All contain Route Itineraries, Route Maps, details of Gradients and Surfaces, Touring Information, Points of Interest, Viewpoints and Scenic Attractions, Location of accommodation, Youth Hostels, camp sites, places to eat and cycle repairers. The suggested cycling routes may be ridden as 'day rides' or linked together to form an on-going tour.

Published by The Riding Press, 62 Sheldon Road, Sheffield, S. Yorks. S7 1GX
Cycling around South Yorkshire.

Available from -
Happy Walking International Ltd., **Unit 1, Molyneux Business Park, Whitworth Road, Darley Dale, Matlock, Derbyshire. DE4 2HJ**

CYCLING Around CASTLETON and the Hope Valley.
CYCLING Around MATLOCK.
CYCLING Around BUXTON
CYCLING Around CHESTERFIELD.
CYCLING Around LEICESTERSHIRE & RUTLAND
CYCLING Around LINCOLNSHIRE.
CYCLING Around NORTHUMBERLAND
CYCLING Around THE LAKE DISTRICT.
CYCLING Around the NORTH YORKSHIRE MOORS - ten routes which provide an on-going tour.
CYCLING Around STAFFORDSHIRE
CYCLING Around the COTSWOLDS
CYCLING Around the YORKSHIRE WOLDS.
CYCLING Around DERBY
CYCLING Around THE ISLE OF MAN
CYCLING around the PEAK DISTRICT - contains eleven routes which may be ridden individually or linked together to form an 'on-going' tour. Details are also given of the popular off-highway Trails.
CYCLING around SHEFFIELD - nine routes in Sheffield's 'Golden Frame.'
CYCLING around HARTINGTON -touring information and route itineraries.
CYCLING around BAKEWELL - touring information and route itineraries.
CYCLING around ASHBOURNE - touring information and route itineraries.
 CYCLING in DERBYSHIRE - eleven of the best cycling routes, mainly in the southern half of the country.
CYCLING in NOTTINGHAMSHIRE - twelve cycling routes which cover most of the county.
CYCLING in the YORKSHIRE DALES, twelve routes which provide an on-going tour
CYCLING around CHESHIRE - twelve routes.

OTHER CYCLING BOOKS from Happy Walking International Ltd.,

PEAK DISTRICT CYCLING - Vol 1 - *Round the bend with Graham* - by Graham Kirkby.
PEAK DISTRICT CYCLING - Vol 2 - *Round the bend with Graham* - by Graham Kirkby.
Four Volumes - CYCLING THE WATERWAYS OF BRITAIN by Philip Routledge.
- Vol 2 - North Midlands and North Wales.